We're the Flow

M000032378

We're the Flownover. We Come From Flyoverland. reveals the splendor—even audacity—that exists in locations and scenes so often not in the center of attention. These expansive poems give quiet, insistent attention ("tuning and tuning") to what might be commonly dismissed as the outskirts, or on the way to noted landmarks. This collection stays in these liminal worlds, whether in the community college parking lot, at a laundromat on a Wednesday afternoon, or waiting to cross Hennepin Avenue at night, where Mauch magnifies them to astonishing, sometimes even damning, insight. Confronting the self and its responsibility, these poems ask: What is my field of vision? How can I step outside of it, change its scope, to witness and "see ourselves / and one another / for what we are"? In *We're the Flownover. We Come From Flyoverland.,* we see a middle America blazing with flashes of beauty, of conviction, and even of resistance.

—Gale Marie Thompson, author
of *Helen or My Hunger* and *Soldier On*

Reading Mauch's work, I'm reminded over and over of Stanley Kunitz's statement that "The first task of the poet is to create the person who will write the poems." Here we have the kind of shimmering lyric insights that can come only from a mind and heart far along the path of enlightenment. What a great gift Mauch has given us by inviting us to share in the journey, offering us no less than "a temple where the door is never locked."

—Melissa Studdard, author
of *Like a Bird with a Thousand Wings*
and *I Ate the Cosmos for Breakfast*

We're The Flowover. We Come From Flyoverland. introduces a roving, Baudelarian speaker seeking to "translate pigeon into English" (the bird's music, or grammatically simplified language), among the streets of "bone and ash," post-empire USA: home to "The Longest Winter on Record." Amid "mirrors not made of metal amalgam and glass," and indexical signs replacing reality ("food we want to eat via pointing"), he mourns the tendency to kill "not the enemy but the messenger," in a world where what's sacred is unprotected: "a temple where the door is never locked." But this speaker is not dissuaded by simulacra nor the steady thrum ("wrong, goddamnit") that "grows into what I hear": instead, he tunes into a "species forgotten," a "small print none have ever bothered to read." The title delivers its promise: the flownover (disregarded) from flyoverland (transcendent) arrive at a Carpe Diem not rapacious but ecstatic, as tourists of the body, in "climax," become those of the mind.

—Virginia Konchan, author
of *Any God Will Do* and *The End of Spectacle*

We're the Flownover.
We Come From
Flyoverland.

Matt Mauch

For Cate —
Copywriter in
a mask — some
poems for
pairing w/ good
food & drink

Matt Mauch

Aug
2021

CONTENTS

In a field of sunlight between two pines,
The droppings of last year's horses
Blaze up into golden stones.

– James Wright

Västerås March 31, 1998

Dear Matthew,

My name is Monica and I am married with Tomas Tranströmer since 40 years. Tomas wants me to write you and tell you that your letter made him happy and he has read your poems. He liked "Turning thirty" very much.

Tomas suffered a stroke which took the mobility in his right side and his speech. The progress is still going on but he can just say a few words today. His understanding is perfect and he has published a new poetrybook. The stroke was of course a tragedy but our life is going on in a good way. Tomas has always been a good amateur pianoplayer, and he goes on with that but now with his left hand.

But he is not surprised that you did not know anything about him but happy that you find him. And he asks you which of his books you have found. And then he say: Matt send me one of your books . . . !

All good wishes from both of us!

Monica Tranströmer

Turning 30 (or 40, 50, etcetera) isn't why

I'm still afraid of the dark. Of night.
And I don't mean death. Don't

mean the fact that I might be single
for the rest of my life. Or buried alive.

Or that my parents will die young
because they've worked hard.

What I'm scared of is a street.
A small town that boasts

nobody has ever been murdered
here. Of walking from the hotel

after a bad interview. After midnight.
Getting lost in an April. In Nebraska.

When a storm kicks up.
And the lights go out. And I'm

where I knew I'd be too soon. Thinking
that I can't remember how old

my brother is. Or his number.
Or my sister's. Or anyone's.

And one wrong step
will trip me over the curb.

When standing still is safest.
That's the dark I mean.

"Livin' on a Prayer"

Half a dryer sheet, not a whole one
is what I overhear. Is what the young mother
angrily whispers to the young father
as their child sleeps, and doesn't. Sleeps, doesn't.

In a laundromat on a Wednesday afternoon
I pile clean, wet clothes in mounds,
draw warm change from my pocket,
feed the dryer its coins.

•

A bowl, if dropped right,
if breakable,

blooms like a flower.

•

Some say
cauliflower is what to say
when you don't know what to say
because your words are on hooks
hanging too high to reach.

They say what they say
about cauliflower
because cauliflower is kind
when you return to it
to try to say what you want to say
all over again.

Cauliflower is also funny, like a friend
almost falling down
in what seems like slow motion,
then pulling out of it just in time

4

without anybody getting hurt.

•

No matter what you say
if you say it in an empty amphitheater,
even if it's an amphitheater
of Maytags,
it grows concentrically larger.

The young mother whispers again.
The young father is folding their clothes
wrong, goddamnit.

•

If the bowl had a stem,
it would follow the dropper's
path

as a tiger lily,
east to west,

follows the sun.

•

I try to focus on Muzak,
on lines I trust to rhyme
that simply aren't there at all.

Wrong goddamnit
grows into what I hear:

that the young mother is about to swim.
That her stroke will be the slow,
crawling-through-time stroke

that Channel swimmers use.

•

With my heart's hands,
I grease the young mother's body.
I whisper *good luck.*

The young father doesn't know
that he's letting down a daughter of Zeus.
That he will not be among her handlers
passing food and drink
by pole
from a boat.

Small, he's made smaller still
by his large mustache. He's trying on
the fathercoat, washing
the impudentcoat, the delinquentcoat, stuck
in a laundromat forever,
like Sisyphus.

•

*That which blooms, then,
is like a dog.*

•

Everything we think of as *other*

has a sense of *we*
in what we, with our own *sense of we,*
think of as its language,

in which we can perhaps count a bit,
say *yes* and *no,*

order a beer,
get beyond that the food we want to eat

via pointing.

•

I draw the last
of the warm change
from my pocket, feed other coins
into myself.

•

> *That which breaks to bloom*
> *its petals of glass*
> *loves you even more than a dog.*

•

I can't remember the words to a song
I thought I had memorized. I'm washing
panties that aren't mine. I'm trying
to become a better man.

Postcard

*From a town of 3,050, where summer culminates
in a day of festivities, the last sanctioned event
being a street dance with a cover band.*

This noon, as every noon,
the steeple bells of the eight denominations

    that we've settled into,
    like particulate,

        ring all at once.

        As if keeping
        cattle at the end of a drive, cops

        all along the parade route

have parked their cars and mounted horses.
The marching band's accompaniment

        tumbles from anthem to cadence,

to echo of a ditty we can't get out of our heads.
We listen like bugs in a jar.

Handbills with the schedule of events
hang in storefronts

        like a refrain.

Blowhole or no, the refrain says *swims.*

    We lean into each other
    like window shoppers
    in the tractor beam of the first TV.

We are swimming too deep.

> Limestone soft,
> we offer our bodies up

> for carving, allow initial after initial
> inside heart after heart

to reduce us to sand.

Trying to decide what I will work
to be reincarnated as

I walk along a shore, look across a lake,
wade in, spread my fingers
so that the curvature of my hands
is inverse to the surface of a rock.
I honorably seize it, tilt it
up from its bed.

Crawfish that were under it
transform into silt, clouds
of used-to-be-here.

I think of the rock
as the sleeping head of a god
I'm gently waking.

Seen through the low-lying gauze
of heat-haze, the sun
is so much smaller than the rock,
is like a gumball
shining through a thin-skinned cheek,
through an old sheet
hung across the sky.

It is hard to think of the sun's light
today as the light of life. It is easy to see it
as tinsel on the thousand tiny waves
I made when I waded in.

Waiting for the fireworks to start

This backyard is Everybackyard,
and I am a kind of Everyman,

       a moving part in a one-day exhibit
       in the natural history of the lawnchair,
       natural history of the officially observed
       bank holiday.

I fix a drink,
lose track of the conversation
in a circle of acquaintances and friends

   unanimous in their public derision,
   their private longing
   for the hot dog, the potato chip.

A bruise-colored pigeon
on a second story window AC unit
coos. I try to understand it

   by cocking my head,
   gathering sound through my good ear,

       same way I'd try to make sense of a question
       asked by a pleasant stranger
       in broken English.

I've nothing to add
to a conversation
   on interior decorating.

       I go in and out,
       translating pigeon, speaking English.

Photos are passed around
of a home for sale
in Florida. I do as the pigeon

suggests: tap the VACANCY sign
on the hotel next door to the house, trace

    features that make it
    for Margaret and me
                a photo of a giant face.

The mothers
go in to breastfeed. The never-have-been-mothers
join them. The slamming screen door
scares my pigeon away.

The new and never-have-been-
fathers, we refresh our GTs, try to coin new slang
for the vagina, something

    with the circumference to eclipse
    twat and *snatch*. Swirling

        ice in our drinks, staring at limes,

we realize that the pigeon
was Everypigeon. And each of us was listening.
And each of us, now, is lost.

Regret is a kind of vest

The setting for wishing
you would have done things differently
might be the banks of a creek
behind a VFW, on the outskirts of town, at 3 AM
on a Tuesday.

You don't have, or need, a Marlboro.
You smoke from a fire within.

The moon is full, hanging like a bulb
in an empty warehouse.

The creek that would be the soloist
singing the ballad
of the end that forgives the means
is bone-smooth, mute.

It's impossible to convince
the dead relatives you answer to
that sending, via thought,
the emotional equivalent
of inflation-adjusted cash
in a security envelope
with no return address
is recompense.

You become your own sentencer.
You're in the belly of an onion.

You touched it as a kid
in the library museum.
Now you know what life is like
lived out in an iron lung.

For the record

I will miss my species when the fate
I've turned away from for so long
is the fate to which I finally assent.

Windows with their shades pulled

on rooms lit in buttery yellow,
rooms lit in jittery blue:

they usher me,
like they're my handlers, like I'm a VIP,

to the edge of town,
where I'm handed over to a field,

where uniform rows of soybeans
turn their leaves to a full moon

which requires them
to also turn their leaves to me.

I feel like a high window

from behind which the faces
that would otherwise casually populate
the canvas of a room
have clustered to look down.

I feel like a whale in air,
like I leapt up and out

and over it all.

Like I got stuck.

Like a constellation
about which

the beans have a story
all beans know by heart, warning

of how easy it is to get sent—

or maybe the bean word
is *sentenced*—

to an eternity
in the sky.

There is so much learning how to be American

See how my steaming sandwich
today is like a geyser? How
my iced soda, next to it, exudes
like a minor vent?

GPS reveals
that I am just off I-29,
not that, from the dispenser,
due to operator error,
I grabbed so many more napkins
than I'll need.

In an older America,
those who could
used to read newspapers
to those who couldn't
like chiefs.

I remember
a short recess from mourning,
the week my grandfather died,
locating and plucking the business
and front-page sections
of the Sunday *Des Moines Register.*
What I wanted was the sports.
I had a Big Mac.

I went from table to table,
half-wall to half-wall,
like a bee doing reconnaissance
in a neighborhood
where the flowers were few
or it was too soon
for them to bloom.

Today I scribble circles
on a sheet of games for kids.

It feels like I'm digging
a hole for a tiny post
which tiny people will use
for something practical
and good.

I tell my pen
that it's my regiment.

I have been to Yellowstone,
the Everglades, the Ozarks,
the Great Salt Lake.

I have not been to Niagara,
Yosemite, the Grand Canyon,
Waikiki, or the Alamo.

I cover my big bills
with ones, and cover my ones
with the fabric of my front right pocket,
as my grandfather did,
my face like a carving at the apex
of whatever I am.

My wallet is a ruse.

I study the profile
on the top of a dime
because my grandfather,
before he lost the cancer weight,
looked like that era
of FDR.

Today I think that they both
also look like a phase
of Paul Bocouse,
and that when I carry them
in my pocket
I'm more robust.

I have been to Mount Rushmore,
to the top of the Empire State,
to the Sunset Strip,
the Smithsonian.

The week my grandfather died
it was river people
who rang the bell
to give us food
like we were the queen bee.

Today I am reading
the Life and Arts
and front-page sections
of a *Wall Street Journal*
I picked like nectar
from in front of a room
I wasn't staying in.

My grandfather read the *Wall Street Journal*
every day. It arrived in the mail, in Iowa,
a day late, which is too late
for it to make you rich.

My grandfather
drove a Lincoln Continental
twice a year
to play craps
on the old Vegas strip.

It was he who taught me
that my wallet
should be a ruse. He said
let pickpockets have it.

He left so many other blanks.

He was buried
with red dice in his money pocket.
I do not know
what I would take with me,
what it is that should mingle
after the conflagration
with my bone and ash.

I have been to the French Quarter
and within viewing range
of the Golden Gate.

Reading the *WSJ*,
I insert myself
into the story leads
like a maid
whose presence doesn't stop
the couple who've rented the room
from continuing.

All of us are drawing slowly
from aquifers.

The amber we'll be stuck in
hardens so swiftly
that we can't prepare a final pose.

It catches some of us
in our sleep.

I unwrap what must be
one of the last plastic straws in use.

My fellow Americans
are all on their phones
learning at the speed of light.

I add drops of my beverage
to the paper that wrapped my straw,

and bring into life
a tiny new mountain range.

I add more drops
and now the tiny mountain range
looks like a backbone.

I want to unzip myself
and wrap around it.

Your children are staring.
I had thought that the fire
was out.

Person of interest 1: How do we know that mosquitos are religious?

Person of interest 2: They prey on you.

Brilliant that we can release into the wild
genetically altered mosquitos

> whose lethal infertility,
> say the scientists in Terni,

will eradicate

> the species itself.
> Eradicating the species itself,

say the scientists in Terni,

> is something we do
> knowing we are killing
> not the enemy

> but the messenger.

Annually killing the messenger
we would save the lives of 400,000 children.

Give or take. Minus or plus.

The war in which mosquitos
are the messengers

> is like the wars
> fought not
> by the conscripted
> but by volunteers.

> For most it is only the idea of war.

While at war we party,
siesta, read,

    tend to our gardens. The Great War taught us
    how to do many discordant things.

It is one of the spoils.
We get it, some say, via DNA.

Why then so few of us
can dance

        as gracefully as our ancestors did?

It has nothing to do with effort.

The densities we hide

I love how my old silver pen
                    is dented where I've tried

to tame it in the teeth,

                    is grooved
                    where the rank-and-file fingers

          have worn
     sickle-shaped paths   as if the metal

     were as amenable to me

as is the wood of my favorite chopsticks.

                    The pen's
                    molten-blue tail

                              all across the page

     is like that of a comet's,

                    stretched out by the gravity

          of more massive things.

I have been unable to train my pores
not to open like portals,

          letting in,
          letting in.

It is why,

               walking out from a basement
               into a sunny day,

my pupils shrink
to a speck.

It is why the rest of me
follows their lead,

in imitation,

says my pen,

*of a poppy seed
that weighs as much as a city.*

Waiting for my car to warm up

The voice on the radio
says the temperature today will dip
gradually below 30, 20, 15,
then tonight below 10.
The voice sounds like it's molting,
like essential parts of wings
are being dropped from it.

I breathe in deeply, am a bag of gas
with the frivolous ability to envision a voice
transformed into a bird.

I breathe out
until I can't breathe out anymore,
until I'm a deflated bag
for tires and shoes
to leave their marks upon.

In the passenger's seat, what I've breathed out
congeals. I say *breath in the shape of a Buddha,*
soak into things,
face what I've said, how I've said it,
then the second congealing: two Buddhas wrestling,
descent into Sumo.

Like a deer
paralyzed by a Subaru's headlights,
I hold my next breath in.

Prior to venturing out, I was reading
from my dead aunt's copy of *Webster's*
Fifth Collegiate Dictionary, flipping
through the "New Words" addition of 1941.
I may as well have been looking at old light
through a telescope, discovering
that prior to my birth
was a time

when I couldn't look up *fiberglass,*
racism, blitzkrieg, jam session,
or *station wagon,*
when if I looked up *stop*
I wouldn't find a definition
of its photographic sense,
a time when *stop*
didn't resemble me in the slightest,

who if I were named now,
in this season of becoming stone,
would be called *Aperture, fair-haired shepherd*
of Penelope's lens, assistant to the god
of exposure, to the god of shapeshifting,
to she of great-hearted light.

Among you

If one were lured by the peppers
growing like suns in pots
on the ledge, and if next one mistook
the open window and lack of glass
for perfectly clear glass, and,
if, furthermore, one leaned in to flatten
a cheek or nose against the cool perfection,
one would fall to one's death.

•

This afternoon I'll drink
the sun tea brewing now in a jar
leeward of the temptress peppers. Like
a species forgotten. Like the small print
none have ever bothered to read.

•

The jar is both dormant, and dominant,
in my view. The blades of grass beyond it
wave like the fingers of baleen
you'll find in a whale's mouth.
I go outside, deep within the belly
of the day, more like a dime passing through
than a grape.

•

I walk with my head down, studying my toes
as they hit their heads on the ceilings
of my shoes. It is as if a row
of burial mounds
were leading the way.

The hard work of life

isn't in the tapping of the true thought.
                    It's in the building a pipeline
                    to deliver the goods.

Having heard third-hand
that an old friend's infant daughter
has died, I call

   and have expensive flowers sent.

An involuntary twitter
in my left cheek, near my good ear,
            is seismic, my geology indicating
        a volcano is underneath.

The refrigerator
isn't saying a thing about food. It's droning
                    a dirge.

I am waiting
for a better way of saying

       Bill, it's been too long.

On the back of papers
a company wants me to fill out
and return, I draw (badly) the underground parts
                    of a family tree.

Without the trunk, etcetera,
my doodle looks like a nest.

Although we know what carpe diem means

We find a seat, become well-packaged humans
on the free bus, wait to depart
from one of the State Fair's
park-and-ride lots.

I tell the woman next to me,
who has taken her heels off, has replaced them
with sneakers and ankle socks,
has locked her valuables in the trunk,
that I heard, on the radio, on the way over,
that the lead singer of a band I saw in a bar once,
and fell in love with,
has killed herself for no good reason.

I say *it's the same reason every time.*

Over the PA loudspeaker,
cutting into a song
I was in-my-head-singing-along-to,
we are told to remember
to hydrate and wear a hat, to report
the unusual, the out-of-place. All signs

indicate that neither the woman
with the afternoon off, nor I,
not having told each other our names,
will be coming away with a story of how we met
on the bus the year the bridge fell.

We've become experts at resisting the temptation
to remove our street clothes, to leap
from building to building
in a single bound, clutching, instead,

the simpler truth of an armrest,
the fact that all we'll be today are bodies fattening up
for winter, mind sacs with a looped

reel repeating *cheese curds, corn dogs, pronto pups,*
Scotch eggs, mini donuts, troutwurst—Oh

beautiful for spacious skies,
land that I sometimes love,
save room for onion fritters, for
pork chops, cheesecake, candy bars,
tater tot hot dish, and bacon,

all of which are served
on sticks, and are eaten
by we who mirror
to mirror see ourselves going on
into infinity, *skewers,*
we think, and lie to ourselves
as we suck our bellies in,
but of a grander sort.

Absentmindedly

I rub my most calloused
hand and finger skin

> against my tended-to
> and smooth-shaven

> face skin,

> fomenting the kind of learning
> in repose

that feels like a new type of high.

I am a student

of a tumbler of lemonade
on the sill

> sweating in rings

>> like a mountain
> rounding off,

rounding down.

> Later today,
> to judge by the trajectory
>> of the moment,

>> the tumbler
>> will become an island

>> one must plan ahead
>> to ferry to.

Much as one turns soil
before seeding

or infects a neutrality
with yeast,

I am preparing

not to sail away
or ship off

but to be gone.

There is a body-mind dualism if I am sweeping
the floor and thinking about Hegel. But if I am
sweeping the floor and thinking about sweeping
the floor, I am all one. Sweeping the floor becomes,
then, the most important thing in the world.
Which it is.

– Gary Snyder

If you see something, say something

Grading Freshman Composition's
required research essay at the community college
in Austin, Minnesota

Yesterday I had to ask
where was I?, having lost my focus
watching a wrist writing
elegant cursive, freed for our time
together from its role
as a wrist that slaughters hogs, gathers
the least obviously usable parts,
stuffs them into blue metal cans,
the cans into cardboard boxes
upon which a machine has stamped
SPAM.

You can make your own bomb
with an empty two-liter bottle
of Coke® or Mountain Dew®,
plus some Draino®
and tinfoil. On its casing
or cone write Anthony Bourdain,
Billy Bragg, RGB,
or AOC.

The bomb is symptom.
The bomb is condition.

In an April that still feels
like winter, the windows steam
when my students meet up
in pickup trucks
before class and their shifts,
on bench seats
with bag lunches,
in the main student lot,
all the engines running.

35

Some say the bomb
is hidden in a garage. Some say
it floats the earth
like a mine.

My students' wrists
write *fuck*
in condensation.
They fill in the blanks
following *fuck*, as if in response
to a question they're sure of.

Regarding the bomb:
has anybody searched
we prisoners' cakes?

Chocolate is the bomb.
Paris is the bomb.
We are the bomb.

My students' wrists
make their way
like worms
into and through
clothes, books, bodies.

Check your backpack.

My students' wrists
are writing and writhing
not fruitlessly, but as the worm
scientists say
fragmentationally.

Fragmentationally
can mean *just because.*
Depending on the tone
you speak it with

it can also mean
now is the time.

**One noncombatant's response
to Operation Desert Storm (or pick
your favorite forever war)**

The morning after the war began
I picked my *Complete Pocket Walt Whitman Anthology*
up from the floor, rescuing it
from beneath the nightstand,
where it was face-down, open,
recovering, like me, from drink.
I blew dust off of the book's spine. Walt
being Walt, I feared the words had gone wild,
were leaking through the floorboards, rafters,
into the apartment below.
Via life-after-death-mouth-to-mouth,
Walter the mother bird fed my abode
a meal of "I Sing the Body Electric."
I turned to the "Drum Taps" section
and, sitting on the toilet,
shined a made-of-air carbine,
packed neat rows of clips
in imaginary ammo boxes, fell in love
with my own voice repeating
nothing new. The next voice I fell in love with,
that very same day, arrived at work,
via telephone, belonging
to Allison from Orion Pictures, Inc.,
who called seeking weekly grosses
for Depardieu's *Cyrano.*
I answered her question:
five thousand sixty-three dollars, no cents.
Then I told Allison that I could see
the miles of open front between us,
the cartographer's pale blue,
pink, and yellow states,
the demarcations fortified
in heavy black, town names
almost too tiny to read,
capitals and county seats

marked by stars. Allison said that she could see
the borderless topographical map. She spent
a full minute describing the marble cake
cooling on her kitchen counter,
the chocolate frosting
lying in wait. We played paper-scissors-rock
on absolute faith.
I hung up the phone
and in a song to myself promised
that if I ever have a kid
I'll name it Allison
or Alvin or Ali or Al,
that my next dog will learn to come,
heel, sit, roll over, play dead, and fetch
to either Walt, Walter, or Wally,
or maybe, if I get a cat,
Miss Whitman.

After a tryst with rain

Untying my laces

      is like untying
      firehoses.

      It provides time sufficient to contemplate
      our footprints

here on earth,

      how they would envy
      if they knew of

          footprints on the moon.

Time to wonder
what kindness the ripe fruit

      I purchased on my errand

            owes the tree

         the rain
         the worker
         the seed,

      the indefatigable role of evaporation
      in the water cycle,

etcetera.

Time to be redressed
as if by Bashō
          saying

          it is one who is not beaming
          who asks such things

                    of fruit that is.

Change

When I read that former San Jose Police Chief Joseph
McNamara said *a corrupt, racist or brutal cop will abstain
from misconduct only when he looks at the cop next to him
and believes that the officer will blow the whistle if he hits
the suspect,*

    I remembered that

    the last time I put a shell to my ear, the Ocean
    (I pissed in sand instead of in it)

    admitted that its consent
    to becoming a poster-child

    for Sweetness & Light

    was given under the duress
    of extortion.

    I told the Ocean
    that I am more afraid of it
    than not.

When I read that an anonymous San Francisco cop said
*when a command staff has a tendency to overlook the
internal infractions or downplay them, they (the younger
officers) see that as support for 'the working cop,' as
protecting the integrity of the organization,*

      I thought of how

      I used to put out food for cardinals,
      goldfinches, chickadees, orioles, jays,

      and with the same hands
      on the same day

pumped up a pellet gun
to shoot at the squirrels

that pilfered the food I put out
for the birds.

When I saw myself seeing myself,
I named the squirrels

and shot the rest of my box of pellets
at paper.

When I read that a second anonymous San Francisco cop
said *the brass doesn't seem to get how disdainful our
community already is of their police, how they see us as a
necessary evil. You can't go to a community meeting and
not feel that venom that so many of these people have
against us, that total disdain,*

I went to a café downtown,
saw people eating alone, across
from empty chairs—
no candlelight, no flowers—

and I thought
that they would have to be birds
with eyes where their ears are
to stare at each other
instead of down

at fork, knife, spoon
wrapped with a napkin
and sealed
with a cuff of orange paper.

I started to introduce myself.
My new acquaintances
did the same.

The quite room
got loud.

    We became birds
    announcing a day
    before we were even sure
    a sun would rise.

The malaise these days

1. The soft and violent *thrrth thrrth,*
i.e., an orange rind tearing.

2. The lubricated gear-grind, terra firma rumble, also called:
buses, passing.

3. The *pank-ity-pank, thooth-fwop*: mail
through the mail slot door.

These are the ordnance aimed
at my embryonic thoughts.
I set my cheeks upon pedestal hands, am forlorn
in its *wandering forlorn of Paris once her playmate*
                                    sense.

I'm like a man in a homburg,
walking with my head down,
stuck in one of the shapes
from the 1930s, when dust
received most of the blame
for the malaise.

Photos at the library capture us
in the involuntary semblances
we fall into after learning
about our manufacturers'
designs for our own
obsolescence. You can find them

in dark aisles where the light
enters only from the side,
where a spleen would be
if a heart were there to feed it, if
the building were a body.

Yesterday, I stared at a photo
with a caption that claimed *The Deepest*

Winter on Record. In it, an unidentified man, his hat
and long coat covering like a tarp,
has just passed the barbershop, eyes down,
so forlornly you could say
forlorn is a sport, that the man's in a zone,

looking earthward,
at his shoes, awed
by them spending their lives
molding themselves
to the bottoms of his feet,
sizing himself up

to about a hundred dollars
or so (they look like good shoes)
in leather, stitching, style.

I stared
until I was no longer there,
until I was subsumed

by a shadow cast
from him and then
to me, which now
is a bridge to you.

Aubade

When the beaver is declared a nuisance animal,
the beaver bounty pays better than hourly wage.

I turn the flashlight down
when I can see well enough
by the blue light
that precedes the day
like a soundless bell. Wind

announces wind.
Fish detonate cover bombs
of silt,

flee upstream
through the creek's claim
in the land.

Water on its pilgrimage
eradicates the murk.
It rings me
like I'm Saturn.

I consider the view from above,
stamp out a nonsensical configuration
in my farmer-friend's field.

I drive stocking-footed,
back to and through a town
just beginning
to stir. I roll
the window down,
switch the heater to high.

Rising from all the houses:
columns of steam in the shapes of bodies,

full and partial nudes, beasts and children,

the armless accepting the fact
of armlessness,

as if the Venus de Milo
were buried beneath us, dreaming
of that which she was made in the image of.

Saying yes to the temptation to

What I thought was
a lovely lingering—

        echoes of my knife
        buttering toast—

                was not that. It was static
                from the kitchen radio

I last remember listening to
three days ago,

when I made pasta
and sauce. I remember

        tuning the radio
        to a singer-songwriter station, singing
        along to "Volare,"

                belting out sounds
                like somebody saved

when I didn't know the words.

                If my life
                is like his life,

that static has usurped
"Volare"

        means the deejay
        must have taken a break

during a longish song. He must have wandered
among the grasses out back.

He believed he was inside a mouth,
was stuck
in a perpetual yawn.

The deejay turned,
sort of ran, found himself

at center
no matter where he turned or ran.

I who used to fear
the coolish lake
of *a cappella*

can hear myself
outside of myself,

    cross-sectioned
    and soft-singing
    "Volare."

I take to a stool.
I take off my boots.
I rub and rub

    my ugly feet.

    I am thinking
    of the feet
        of statues.

I am ready to flare up and become a radar blip

There is nothing free
about an intersection
with a mailbox, a church,
a hydrant.

        Of the lone empty corner?

There I am a green tomato
in late October, left on the vine,

            insufficiently ripe,
            the gardener thinks,
            for salad, sauce,
            or soup,

      too green and hard
      to boil and skin,
      to can or freeze
      for winter use.

I do not want to be useful

I want to stop making
my way through the day

like I'm a shim. Want to forget about the mallet
driving the shim.

I want to stop being
so low to the ground. Want to feel

less like an udder
with nothing left to give,

no memory
of grip pull twist squeeze,

how it lets the inside out.

I want to climb the tallest tree I can find,
to the highest branch

able to hold my human weight.
I want to encourage the slenderer branches

higher up: *Prick the firmament.*
Bleed down a sample of beyond.

I want to unfocus
my gaze, blurring the orange and yellow leaves,

the few trees still green, softening the world,
merging the seldom merged,

valley and city and river reclining
like paint-spackled nudes.

I want to channel the Gustav Klimt
Gustav Klimt always wanted to be,

to turn osprey, owl, or crow, marveling

at the surprising ease of flight, joints
cracking in places where I never imagined
I could bend.

As if orders had come down

The moon tonight
has landed on and blocked the road ahead of me,
                                acting more Jupiter
                        than moon.

                I look left, right.

The night is a room.
It has been wallpapered
by Maurice Sendak!

The road is like a carpet rolled out. The moon
is pregnant with my favorite star's light.

                The pregnant light
                is bleaching Maurice Sendak's trees!

I pull over, park, and get out.
I leave the car door open,
key in the ignition.

If the moon abducts me, the finders
of abandoned things will think *what happened*
happened quick. This was an emergency.

I kill a mosquito.
I am sorry for what I have done.

I breathe in what the night
exhales. It's like I'm making out
        with lilacs.

I sit with my back against a tire,
then get on the hood,

                absorb the engine's heat
                until I feel like the one solid thing

at the heart of a nebula.

I get down from the hood clumsily.

I'm always forgetting
I inhabit a mass
others can see.

I put my head back, settle into the contours
of the ditch.

Everything would be different
if I had never read that the pull
of the right kind of body,

in the right conditions, given time, is enough
to draw many other things
to its center.

It would be different
if I could hear the moon
saying anything other than *take
an inventory. Invent a tool.*

Luminescence

I'm stuck
trying to cross Hennepin Avenue
at night,

when it's varnished with rain,
is dyed by lights
from clubs and commerce
so that it looks
like a Turkish rug.

I'm like the chicken
who's just been told the joke
about the chicken
crossing the road
and doesn't get it.

In the middle of the street,
car horns
and city noise converge
to make song, like
they're following a score.

I feel like a surgeon
standing over an open chest,
expected to impose
order upon a heart,
which, when you're close in,
and it's dying,

transfixes
like a blossom
unfolding
in a time-lapse film.

Middle of the street.
Heart of the city.
The incandescents, fluorescents,

and neons wonder aloud
if I remember where it was
I was in such a hurry to get to.

I am a temple where the door is never locked!
This despite the gun violence of our times!

I am housing
framed things, bolted things,
things with padded seats, lacquer, handles,
and lathe-spun legs!

> I am housing
> things that require electricity
>
> or if not that
> light!

I am housing that which will perish
without my husbandry
and management of resources!

If I feed you after cooking
something up

> with some of the ingredients
> I house, I will you ask you
> how it tastes!
>
> > All of my questions
> > come out of me
> > as koans!
> >
> > There is no
> > agenda-setting!
>
> Answers are something
> I have tried to but cannot house!

I am paid as well as any housewife!

Abandonment, fire,
redevelopment!

The winding down! The lean
of entropy!

    High winds!
    A need for more space
        for crops!

So many things to house!
So many new ways to die!

There are mirrors not made of metal amalgam and glass

I walk beneath an elm
that didn't catch Dutch elm disease,
an elm I should learn from, elm the crow
that calls the shots

dubbed *the* tree, announcing *this
fits our number, is our roost.*

I walk across the litter of crows
splattered on the sidewalk
like a bridge of stars.

I'm not shat on
why?

The crows are telling me I can swim
in the sky like it's a sea, that paths
are being revealed
right now, that one's

movement through it, the reaching out and cupping
of a handful, the strong return, the twist,
the lift and reaching again—you don't

need water
yet swim is exactly
what you do.

At night,
I listen for heads being tucked under wings,
for breathing though feather masks.

It should be easiest to keep track
of the business of crows
after it snows.

It snows. What's easy to see
is that the air rights of crows
supersede
those of the city.

The elm's
a bouquet of wire. The crows are leaving it
one by one.

If I'm translating crow sign correctly,
what this means
is that there will be times

when we'll need to give each other
more elbowroom
than we imagine
we can,

and not being crow,
we'll have to do it like contortionists,

within the confines of a patio
or bedroom, or what's even more likely

is that everyone will gather in the kitchen,
and it's there that we sardines,
who like to pretend we're whales,

will see ourselves
and one another
for what we are.

The plot

It gets more and more
jarring,

      the body parts
           that seem to fit

the glass slipper best.

               Then in slides

      the better-fitting
      mind!

As if we are a mountain.
As we are free climbing

      ourselves.
      A UNESCO-cited

             optical illusion!

Interspersed
are scenes

        of a tourist
        trying to refold a map

    along the original creases.

Tourist in a lobby,

        in a car,
        at the market,

      in the cathedral,
      at a cash machine.

In the best-case
scenario,

        in the early shots
        the tourist is the body.

        By the climax,

the tourist is the mind.

In the place of a denouement

is a shot of the map
crumpled in the trash.

        In the first cut
        it was a shot

of the slipper.

SOS

*After morning reading on the imbalances
between new and old in reconstructed Nagasaki.*

The lawncrew my neighbor has employed
puts the equivalent of a cherry atop the sundae
of its work:

a sign that says
for 48 hours
kids and dogs
shouldn't play here. I hold out

my palm like a bridge,
across the property line,
to a death-sentenced milkweed plant,

to a caterpillar
that crawls from the underside of a leaf
onto my hand, goes back and forth
from hand to hand.

I look into its caterpillar face,
try to eye-to-eye tell it
that I, too, am naked
and seeking the shade

of window boxes, ledges, handrails,
mailboxes, shelves.

I, too, feel the urge
to cocoon
or chrysalis.

As in a bedtime story,
I tell the caterpillar
that I will sort-of save it, will carry it
into my space,

64

from which it may emerge as a monarch
or a swallowtail, living
a life that will feel like pleasure boating
in a yacht with a full-time crew.

Thing to thing, I whisper
that most of us unfold
as day moths, that the days
tend not to feel like pleasure boating.

Most of us, I whisper,
are navigating the chops and swells
in a drug-runner's skiff.

But there's overage, and I tell the caterpillar
that, because they keep saying,
because I keep hearing
the truth will set us free.

We were here

The Neanderthals wrote their histories
in soft wood, passed along their cosmologies
in gesture.

Me, I'm trying to do something
as ephemeral as that
for the inventor of the red light,

for the genius conceiver
of the DON'T WALK sign,
for the seconds ticking down,

the time they've given me
to figure out that *city,*
rightly considered, is a contraction
of *gravity.*

Time to wonder
if after death we're allowed
to crowd the one-consciousness kiln,
to mob the gates,

or if we must go in an orderly fashion,
one at a time, no assurance

lovers will and enemies won't
be fused together.

I feel best understood
by the off-colored stone
set among the same-colored rest

at the top center of a building
where the builder,
rather than leaving a name, etched
only 1883
into its face.

I cross the street,
address a partly cloudy sky
with only my eyes, ask

how many of us
must be melted down
and melded together
to make a single brick?

My toes in my shoes
in my socks
attempt the midair pose
made famous by cliff divers
on postcards.

Take a countenance
and remove its skull,
you have something
like a building façade.

Next to a revolving door's
hydra of bullet-proof tongues,
face to face with a building
ready to eat me, I kiss

a brick warmed by sun,
just to taste it.

As in birding, the distinctive sounds we make count as a sighting

*When one finally receives
the samizdat!*

I pick out
the blades of grass

that, like rivers
before they enter the sea,

or like malleted meat
hung to cure,

are flat and wide enough
to hold between my thumbs,

next to my lips.

I blow and elevate them
to reed.

Of the four acknowledged stages
of translation,

two are now complete.

Next something happens
in the siphoning canal
of the ear.

If a tickle,
be tickled.

This is how the prodigal joy
that you thought was extinct

returns from sojourn.

Tra la la

        la la la la,

   tra la la

la la la la.

Only one sweeter end can readily be recalled—
the delicious death of an Ohio honey-hunter,
who seeking honey in the crotch of a hollow tree,
found such exceeding store of it, that leaning
too far over, it sucked him in, so that he died
embalmed.

– Herman Melville

The lullaby and well of night visit the day
most memorably in things as resilient as wool

As in the ecstatic and pastoral traditions,
wool is still insulative when wet.

There's an itch across my back.

Black wool follicles
grow conjoined though glad pores,

blanket of wool cocooning
me as I croon: O,

there's not enough praise for wool,
black wool.

I can't bring myself to scratch the itch.

An enormous ebony spider
has spun and is spinning
the universe.

The Milky Way's stuck
like a bug.

Are you lounging
in your dreams
in pasture with your arms
around the shoulders

of the getting naked-er
as we get hairy-er
donor sheep?

Black wool is teaching
the flownover

in flyoverland.

73

Wrap your eight legs
around me. We'll sleep like the jailed,
          on sheets of wool, sleeping the sleep
          of black wool sheep,

                    like dead pharaohs
                    or worms
                    tunneling through them.

How chosen-one
to give up
this for that, to embrace

a worm's or pharaoh's
caste, rejecting wine, song, knives, spoons,
trumpets, bunting, guilt—

                    sleeping eternal black wool sleep—

no infernos, beatitudes, treasures,
boots, alarms, or rain

to wake us up. I kiss black wool,
                    turn it into trousers,
                    flames, leaves, spin
                    ruby-black wool

          into black wool I—

                    at ten below zero, a halo of wool
          protects my brain
                    from frostbite.

I shovel an eight-inch snow
from woolen steps. It's like shoveling
eight inches of dead skin
after an eight-day angel orgy.

To become woolen
is to emerge from underground
caked in earth.

It is like being endowed
with a black wool bullshit detector!

Hatched from wool
is a bird who hears things

at the decibel level of melting snow. It flaps
its wings so fast

it seems wingless, its beak in the lead,
tearing into what's next.

A black and woolen rope
drops from what you might call

up there.

I reach for it. A dog that wants it as much
growls at black wool I,

a gray and yellow-haired dog
raised on scraps of wool

dragging its shadow
and in the shadow, which is seething:

the steam engine,
the wheel,
the formula for maintaining orbit.

This shaggy-haired and stray olive dog
carries the repentant morning sun

on its mutt-gray back.

Hold velvety black, prismatic hologram wool
to the light

       and turn it, redirect
       the light to the street

       where traffic stops
       for what has the feel
       of an accident:

              a black woolen wrecker,
              an ambulance,

flashing emergency lights. Waiting for word,
everyone's tapping woolen feet.

       A black blues ditty
       is played at the speed of

barbed-wire
blood-black
wool.

              The dead make a stew
              with steel, glass, and plastic
              as the broth.

                  From the bowl of the night
                  I eat the stew
                  using an every-drop spoon.

       Who robbed the cricket of hair?
Hey, cricket, take some of mine.

       The spider has hair. There's
       the hairy fly. There's partaking
       of hairy me.

Cricket must have hairs

I can't see with a woolen lens.

What I can see: the almost-clogged heart
in a creek-bed pebble,

trout
using their hands,
spinning a black wool tunic.

They could raise a barn
if they wanted to

these trout

dancing an underwater
half-out-of-water
dance,

a black wool ballet.

It's raining wool, black wool. Woolly cricket,
make a C note with your one leg awkward
against mine.

A globule of hail
falls past my window, collides with pavement,

makes twelve less-significant globules of hail

that dance like mad scientists

racing to invent a black wool umbrella.

Tomorrow, at 8 AM,
drinking black wool coffee in my kitchen,
steam and nose hair mingling,

I'll belch black wool
out an open window,

                              winning the race.

That either the X's or O's

                 and not both
                 must carry the game

is sad

                 but is not the saddest
                 song you'll hear.

                         When I was eating my own tail,

I was a black-wool dervish, was
soil too deep to be frozen,

                 boiling up into snow-cover'd fields.

                         A cloud fills up.

                 Pavement cracked by roots
                 is also stained by leaves,
                 is clearly disrespected
                 by trees.

My footprints in snow
                 expose the snow's Achilles heel.

I am both
the slow water beneath the frozen river
                         and the man rolling bread into balls
                 to use as bait for carp.

                         Fix me a drink, a stiff one.

Touch lightly the crack through which neon
has seeped, and you're touching

                              78

me, saboteur of signs.

Dear echo of bells: talk with me
who am what seems like inadequate root structure
                for a heavy trunk.

                        Despite me, the tree thrives.

Sea foam bogarts the beach.

The needle weeps for a pulled-out stitch. The lamp
not plugged into a wall

        is my model for bravery.

        It's true that I sold what was stamped
        SOUL

                to the Johnny Appleseed of bridges,

                        our transaction taking place
                        in the pungent air
                        above the imprint of a hoof
                        in mud.

In the dilated pupil of steam,
we possessed all-encompassing sight.

                I could see the coins
                inside the opaque pockets
                of the just-dead,
                how, more than warm,
                they were almost hot.

I could see that a leak in the forest ceiling
was responsible for the balance of hawks,
                the graffiti of wind.

I bent to the gospel of apes,
crossed the country
on the exoskeletons of pioneer hope,
cresting hill after hill.

O black woolen fingers,
pollinate!

> Star light, star bright, star of black wool night:
> I almost passed out in the shower.
> I spat out what tasted like the bad,
> settled on my knees.
> The distance from my lips
> to the showerhead
> was insurmountable.

I believed I could breathe through my hands.

On a floor that feels like the ocean
floor, I have what feels like a blowhole.

> I crouch and kick
> from three, from
> > seven miles deep,

> > burst through knitted waves,
> > over sailing boats,

trailing sea goo,
smudged with woolen residue.

> > I also see myself
> > as a cell under a microscope

> with a bunch of other cells.

Come with a torch.
> Switch to a match

when you're close. The night

is holding forth,
      night speaking.

         It has a million
         other things to say.

Human speech is like a cracked kettle
on which we beat out tunes for bears to dance to
when we long to move the stars to pity.

– Gustave Flaubert

Perfect

Before Lou Reed was
Lou Reed in my rearview mirror,

I saw him from what would be considered
a bad camera angle,

in an aisle where I couldn't find

my cheese, where all I could make out
from behind

was male, dressed head to toe in black.

Now I see
sunglasses, curly hair, the signature thin line
    of an upper lip, and I wonder most

not why he's in St. Paul
but why he's chauffeurless,

is driving a Chevy. In
my bag I have bread, juice, bananas,

tomatoes, fish, and rice.
I have taken advantage

of an end-of-summer sale
on locally grown,

over-ripe cantaloupes. I turn

left and watch Lou Reed
turning right. What I may or may not

do next is go out and buy
all of his records at the used stores

just because of this.

Tonight, when I eat my melon,
I'll wield a spoon

like it's the key that unlocks me, answers
whether I'm organic

or android,

eating and singing
I thought I was someone else,
someone good, you made me forget,
what a day.

On the day before Labor Day

I find myself,

before the side dishes and dips
I've promised to make
are made,

pissing in cattails,
one eye closed,
because sometimes

I piss that way, surveying
half of all I can see.

Being from here
makes me the product
of a people who use all the land
they can

to grow soybeans and corn.

I open the closed eye,
because sometimes
I piss that way, too,

and see that being from here
also means
I'm the product

of strategically placed tree lines
and groves,

of a people who suffer wind.

If I could be a body of water
rather than one comprised
mostly of it,

if I were skinned, de-boned,
dispersed,

I would like to be a slough
overgrown with wild reeds,
wild rice, bulrushes.

Prior to the beak-on-wood
drumming of a downy woodpecker,
sessioning

with a willow and grubs,

I had convinced myself
that I wanted to become
an ocean. Pissing,

I've sunken
an inch at least,
or two, into mud, becoming

more or less
what I am.

A post for the Classic Mopar Forum

At 81 miles per hour
on interstate highway something or other

                  headed south, I tuned and tuned
                  the radio dial

      in a car
      the vinyl seats of which
                and vinyl appliqué

            along each side

      and its hood medallion
      and bench seats

were all emblazoned
with a design

based on the Aztec eagle.

      Two or three hundred

           flocked around me,
           both cradling

and leading.

      It was a kind of call
      and response.

           A nestling into.

      An autopilot.

Tuning and tuning, I was trying
to make a connection

back to the old GE console

that was as dominant
in the living room I grew up in

as a box car

or as a mausoleum
in New Orleans

or Pere Lachaise.

A console
in which The Beatles,
etcetera,

were interred,

walking beheaded,

in profile.

What I finally tuned in
was an edition of myself
swaying

in front of the console,

in blue pants and a white shirt,
muddied to the nipples, like

a reenactment
of Chicken Little's
falling sky.

The road, polyrhythmically,
was elevated

and escorted me

and itself

     was escorted

     by ditches to either side
     earning

rivers of their own.

I was not
driving but sailing.

I was not sailing
but sailed over.

     Beyond the evergreens

     oil derricks
     may have been pumping.

     Graders may have been stripping
     the land.

I was a waterplant.

Pretty and oblivious.

Twenty-three and broke.

Suitable for a marriage alliance.

A fish on sacrifice day.

Charting apexes

Even one

who is native

to the plains

finds oneself drawing

a mountain range.

This is an ode

High schoolers
flood the neighborhood I live in
every afternoon
at three. They speak

> so openly to each other
> it is as if the distance
> from last class to car
> provided an immunity

like the one you get
from high dive
to splash.

> They are more than ready

> > for summer
> > in the sense
> > that summer
> > is humid air imbued
> > with lilac incense
> > lasting forever.

They're as suspicious

> of men like me
> who aren't at our jobs

> > as birds are
> when a new feeder's fresh from the box,
> full of foreign seed.

> > I use
my *Mutual of Omaha's Wild Kingdom*
> overdub voice

to say to an audience

of house plants and a cat

that while the high schoolers
may seem simply to be givers and getters
                    of a ride home,

            their interactions
            are wildebeestean-crocodilean
                            at heart.

            Both
            givers and getters
            swear in inventively
            vulgar spurts, funnel

past our houses
so quickly

that rather than fertility
            they leave dry gulches
            in their wakes.

For the plants, who have proven
            easier to captivate
            than the cat, I rise

            in defense of the givers' and getters'
            use of *mother-cocksucking, shitpouch-licking
            horse-fucker.* They are trying

to tell men like me
who have a midweek day off,
or who work from home,

                    or who don't work at all—
                    gone DIY in garages,
                    front yards, on ladders,
                    as fixated on our spheres
                    of influence

as are raccoons
who smell salmon
in a dumpster battened down—

that while we may have
a vision

of a pink and silver meal,

we've forgotten that claws
are the only tools we need.

So much precedes the end stop

It's no longer late at night.
It's early in the morning.

            I am
diaphanous, as milky and firm
as sweet corn

        pre-boil, ear witness

to eight automobile tires
arching their spines
into concrete

            at an intersection
            sixty-odd paces
            from my box seat,
            my still life.

I reach for my shoes. A reflective
yellow center line
splits the hemispheres
in my cranium.

Mid-reach,
I become a frieze
on a temple to a god of luck.

This is during the transfer of momentum
to the bodies. This is when a wave

            carries from my skull
            to the intersection,
            then back.

            This is my belief, for three full seconds,
            in escaping souls.

This is road paint
swallowing stop-and-go lights.

It is the distillation
of scream to sing.

As if it were always so

Thinking of Pompeii,
of 79 CE.

Pheasant tracks

      like tiny naked trees
      in a Yuan mindscape

          climb each other

like those caught
forever trying
      to survive, over-

          printed each
          upon each in snow

just fallen,

      the outreached
      making up an infrastructure

          upon which

I crowdsurf.

      They made of glass.

          Me their flag.

Planted in a wind
that is no wind at all.

Transacting

I earn money
so I can pay the daughter
who speaks English for her seamstress mom
ten dollars for a five-dollar patch job
on a pair of jeans I've been fixing
for twenty years.

The politics
implied by the Levi's
are not my mother's. In the matter of underwear,
mom counseled me to buy new yearly,
to throw out favorites if they're ragged,
worn thin, said I wouldn't want
a rumor of shoddy briefs
to make it to the nurse's station, to become
they are ill-mannered, know no better,
are probably poor.

My mother's advice on underwear
as a correlative to reputation and namesake
is one example of a theme, a doctrine
from behind which a nation never emerges
in a cold war that lasts forever.

Like a chorus line of block letters lit at night,
all night long, is the girl's family name,
from which, once a week,
she scrubs off
the pigeon and sparrow shit.

Today the family O
has let its petals out. Today
I give her money. She gives me jeans.
She tries to give me money back.
I close my fist. With small, strong fingers
she tries to open it.

She's a kind of sun.
She has recognized
that my fist
is a bud.

In reply

Sun eats fog leisurely. We're close to the river. It's morning. I point out the usual: pheasants, deer, turkey, afraid of it all, crouching in the ditch, tiptoeing at the edges of fields. I point out the opposite of the usual: hawk after hawk after hawk, who may be undercover police. "A bounty of hawks," I say to my imaginary traveling companion, modeled after an ex who insisted I name her tongue. A second imaginary companion modeled after a one-nighter who was more like an eighth-of-a-nighter, that eighth-of-a-night accountable ultimately for ending whatever I and the ex who made me call her tongue "animal" had—this fling who wanted to do it in the front seat at the fairgrounds after the midway closed, and when I declined offered a menu of alternate places and ways to get off, most of which I also declined, thinking of how I'd hurt the ex not yet an ex—as she did then, she does now, piping up from the back seat with "a fruit of hawks."

It takes four minutes and ten seconds of hard thinking disguised as singing along to Madonna's "Crazy for You" before I can say of a hawk perched on mile marker 141, "It reminds me of a catalog model, the feathers like a pressed shirt and tailored suit, like it belongs in an ad." The ex, who is riding shotgun, who has had the cute vestigial skin tag she always swore she'd lance off lasered off, throws in with "an occurrence of hawks," which I almost don't hear, wishing I could draw the skin tag back in. The fling who had me more than I ever had her in those 75 minutes that have stretched into years, whose cigarette and sandpaper Demi Moore circa *St. Elmo's Fire* voice is as compelling and dangerous as the razor knives knife swallowers ask a member of the audience to touch, says, "A confluence of hawks." A third imaginary traveling companion, who in the aftermath of what happened with the fling and the ex dressed *I love you* in the late-80s slang version of *no strings attached*, joins in, joins us, says, "a gathering of hawks."

I point to a hawk on a wooden post, hawk that appears to be guarding a field of wheat. I say, "It reminds me of a political underdog, a long shot on election night memorizing two speeches as the results trickle in." As earnest and misunderstood and over-taught as a tour guide, I say that the highway we're driving follows more or less the overlap where the Mississippi and Central Flyways merge. The assembled imaginaries know me well enough to expect that in less than 24 hours I will look up and report that the two official names for a group of hawks are "kettle" and "cast." I should but do not know whether hawks migrate or whether these have simply taken advantage of the other birds' instincts to follow a path. The one who like me has yet to move on, chimes in with, "An opportunity of hawks." Near Topeka we see what ends up being the last hawk of the day, drenched in pink and orange, the sun a blooming coal.

Turns out an eighth of a night, when I recalculate to include months-later skinnydipping, is selling the fling short. I acknowledge an eighth of a night plus. She says, "A feed of hawks." I say, "If we're anything like the migratory birds, we'll winter as least as intimately as guests in adjoining rooms." At a gas stop in Oklahoma, I leave the imaginaries, except for Hegel, in the car. The clerk taking my money for a chocolate bar asks her companion clerk in the middle of my transaction if she noticed the hawks coming through. Waiting for Hegel, perched like a parrot on my shoulder, to reveal the self-evident, I say, "The last one I saw looked like the bud of a flag, where a brand new and better country, with an amazing constitution, available in PDF, wished it could begin." I count to ten. "We should," I say, "spend every dollar we have translating the ceasefire that the birds agree to in the south." Hegel says he'll meet me in the car. Dar (if her name tag is really hers) doesn't touch my hand when she gives me my change, saying without saying *mister, what planet are you from?*

A helium-filled Mylar happy face

that got away

      when not enough attention was paid,

           smiling as it rises to the tropopause,

makes me believe
that Icarus would do it again,

           that I

      would do it for the first time,
      knowing

what I know
notwithstanding.

**When as a young man I rented a place
for a year or so on one of the streets
that serves as a border for Eatonville, Florida**

I crossed the street.
I went looking for Zora Neale Hurston,
for light in the canopy of an old oak,

something I could reasonably say,
the way it drips
from pools on leaves,
had inspired a page I've read.

What I found
was an old woman rocking.
The porch the woman rocked on
had gone so far downhill, to seed,
the wood so gray and smooth
I bet (I thought) *it's petrified.*

Did she stand,
via Zora, and take
a broom in her hands,
herding the debris the afternoon storms
leave like a deposit at the bank,
as if she owned
not only the weather
but the sky?

Did she hike up her dress,
kick off her shoes,
lift a bare foot in judgment,
aiming for my heart,
intending to rip through bone,
clench my blood with her toes?

She stood. She swept.

Like Frankenstein to his monster

A photo of the last flowering
                    of the intermittently

                    and night-blooming cactus

is what I keep in a cheap frame
next to the intermittently

            and night-blooming cactus itself.

I've given the cactus the ledge
that catches the best light,

            have set it

            in a pot made of papier-mâché, pot
            that over-watering, overflowing

will disintegrate, making it
a pot that saves us, reminds

                    of the perils
                    of too much, warns

of drop-offs, drowning,
swimming at our own risk.

            I tell the cactus the truth:

that there are boys and girls everywhere
touching their better selves.

        Touching one's better self,
        I say, is its own kind of blooming.

It's a borrowing from
for which one never owes.

Lost

Having failed to find the bar

with the orange moose out front,

I stop to watch
a fisherman

or fisherwoman   or fisherperson

or god in disguise

I can't tell from this

distance

reeling something reelworthy in.

I root for all sides   roll the window down

tell Odysseus I have no idea

what gifts I owe to the bringer of the lovely breeze.

Not being Ojibwe   I don't have permission

to ask the Ojibwe spirits

for anything.

But I do.

My Marquis Brougham has ruptured
its lower radiator hose

On the gravel shoulder,
on the east side of Highway 60,
south of Bigelow,

I see close up,

as if walking
through a microscope's tube,

that half or so of the rocks
are dirty-goose white

and the other half
are desert-soldier beige.

Mere minutes ago

as seen through window glass
at a rate of sixty-plus
miles per hour,

as if on special exhibition,

the stones,
Van Goghing, seemed

to me to be a monochrome
marble slab.

Between one sign
welcoming me to *a place to grow,*

and a second
poking at the first
with its claim of plentitude—
land of 10,000 lakes—

I am uncounted, unknown.

      It is as if the secrets of some trade
      are being revealed
                  to me,

            right now,

while my fellow conferees
are all at lunch out,

      identifying one another
      by their lanyards.

I am an emissary for myself.

      The gravel dust I kick up

      follows me
      as I am enveloped
           by it.

           Like it's moor fog
           Like I am its protagonist.

    I shade
sun from my eyes. I salute
my welcoming party

      of one:

      a meadowlark
      with its toes curled,

           as if grasping
           a branch of air
           in specimen mode
           in a lab,

or playing dead
on a stage,

      the magician's assistant
      practicing the pose it must hold

to be sawed in half.

As with paper folded along various creases and turned into a flying machine

Despite a cap of clouds
the color of iron
that can't or won't
          rain,

my shadow shows me as sparrows
mating midair.

Shadow, I have positioned my body
at such an angle to the day
          as to yield

your twelve-foot rendition
of deaf-mute me.

I make you do the robot
winding down,

losing charge slowly,
head staring at empty hands.

Shadow, a whiskey glass,
after surviving

the Korean War, Sputnik, Integration,
and Nixon

in my grandfather's cupboard,
          in his grip,

just broke
as I was drying it
with a thin white cloth.

I lean against a wall.
My shadow assumes the position

one assumes
for frisking.

My feet are as heavy as a bear's.

I make my shadow reach
for something

      like fruit.

#bouillabaisse

Bluegills are known to strike on a bare hook.
A school of them will eat six times its weight
in a summer.

We are the temporary stars
of the surgical theater.

There is no magnetism.
No flirting.

We rendezvous

> where the water
> and air
> are too clear
> to yet be even
> the subtlest broth.

It is testing theories, tying
to my line all
the shininess I can find.

Remember:
we must never come
to a boil.

> The crow
> in the loge is seated
> and waiting.

> The crow's pleasure
> is like the pleasure of one
> with no expectations.

See the line that shows
where we were,
and how we've reduced?

This is how we fit
into their spoon.

A bomb on Garfield Ave (we're all fiddling)

I have sketched and labeled *Figure 1.*

       Wood Piece A. Wood Piece B.

       Male and female parts.

       A core of air.
       A tunable reed.

              Connecting the female A
              to the male B

              is implied.

                          As is song.

    •

I sketched *Figure 1*
over an unlabeled and erased sketch
of sonar seeking giant squid.

              Invisible tendrils
                   to visible ones.

    •

I memorized the first sketch.

I am passing this second one along.

    •

If you drop the instrument in *Figure 1*
from a height,

as you must to hear its song,

114

falling it looks more like Little Boy
than Fat Man.

•

The *X* in the diagram
stands in for the number of times
I have lit a fuse long enough
to not know the damage done.

•

Any empty or vastly
underpopulated piazza-
ish place,

        say the ocean
        with its ship
        or two like seabirds

                at the drop-off,

is a good place to wait
for the promised song.

Much as one waits for belief.
Notwithstanding

that if I am the test case,
the trial study,

        the astronaut
        on a craft not slated
        to return,

my inclination is to announce
that there is no good place to wait.

•

(waiting)
We will feel thinned out from the mother plant.

•

Over and over
is the primary game.

The piece we play it with
is one from which we have to remove

moles at the dermatologist's behest
when we and the dermatologist

land on the same square.

•

Like a stone gargoyle in 1882
whose view of the conflagration
(while waiting along with us for the song)
was best save for the view
of certain birds

       but today has dropped on the list
       below choppers and drones
       (and still the birds),

what we learn and will wish to teach
about waiting and song
we will have to teach to the children of the future
in the language of souvenir.

•

(waiting)
I feel like a cartoon aardvark

in a tux.

(waiting)
I remember being able to rewire
the faultiest of night skies,

bringing my skill to the city,
finding it of little worth.

(waiting)
I remember we are filters
but I am trying to understand
why some say *mainly.*

(waiting)
I peel off
my most prominent scar
        as if my skin were a bandage.

                The tissues in the muscles
                below the scar
                reveal themselves
                to be letters held by an old rubber band.

                Touched gently and with reverence,
                like an antiquarian book, the rubber band
                disintegrates.

                One is free to read what the letters say
                as they stretch their limbs.

(waiting)
One becomes the spider
        welcomed into a strange house

                per the example set
                by Kobayashi Issa.

    •

Waiting we are vortex.

I.e., a vacuum is created
when we breathe in.

As is a balloon.

    •

Waiting we are like the lenses we concoct
to see television, print, and space

                     more clearly through;

we have come from opacity;
it is *such* a journey.

    •

The fallout?

        It anthropomorphizes
        everything.

Untitled

Charting apexes
requires one to also
chart valleys.

Passing the laundromat (at Grand and 36th),
like Frankenstein the monster [sic]
to Frankenstein the creator, I
am mostly lost.

It is as if I have ruptured
something as vital
as a radiator hose.

A helium-filled Mylar happy face
is showing a way.

Turning 30, then 40, then 50,
etcetera, is why I know all the words
to "Livin' on a Prayer"
by heart. Is why I send postcards
explaining what I am working
to be reincarnated as.

It is why I want to play you
at Trivial Pursuit.

On a sunny morning at
the end of the Year of the Jittery Heart,
a young man rents a place
on one of the streets
that's the setting
for a bunch of old stories
and books
he's still reading
long after their author has died.

As if orders had come down,

he thinks he is a temple
where the door is never locked.

Waiting for the fireworks to start
(it was New Year's Eve),
he understands that regret
is a kind of vest. For the record?
He thinks that there is too much learning
how to be American.

#He is among you.
#He knows what carpe diem means.

Person 1 asks Person 2: How do we know
that mosquitos aren't religious?
Or that we see the same thing
when we say we see blue?

#So much precedes the end stop.
#As if it were always so.
#Oh the places you can go
waiting for your car to warm up!

There's an 'A' bomb on Wardour Street.
There's an 'A' bomb on Garfield Ave.
We're all fiddling
and not.

#If you see something, say something.
#Say it in an aubade
to add the Romeo and Juliet-ish
urgency of separation.

I have no daughter, no son.
I am like paper
folded by somebody else
into my shape.

After a tryst with rain

I do not want to be useful
anymore.

#bouillabaisse
is what I want.

I am but one noncombatant
and my stock response
is to say yes to the temptation to.

#In reply.
#The malaise these days.
#The lullaby and well of night
continue to visit the day
most memorably in things
as resilient as wool.

There are mirrors not made
of metal amalgam and glass.
The plot, the luminescence, the SOS:
this is how we say we were here.

As in birding, the distinctive sounds we make
count as a sighting.

#Perfect day.
#This is an ode.

Slow mo on the morning of New Year's Eve, at the end of the Year of the Jittery Heart

for Kwame Dawes

Jittery heart, is it that you have already
said your say?

                    You are quiet
                    as the dead
                    today,

          amidst the practicality
          of tree trimming, winter

                    like an X-ray revealing
                    good bones and bad,

                    which to keep
                    for posterity,
                    which for good luck
                    to amputate,

to stack and burn
so we can think through smoke—

                    common incense,
                    common ceremony—

     of the dead
     who seem yet
          to be steering.

          Like many practicalities,

                    the tree trimming
                    is also a politics, the limbs

                    to be sacrificed hanging

122

over the property of one,

belonging to a tree
rooted in the property of a neighbor next door,

the bartering and quid pro quo
that keep my neighborhood from war

not investigated, not reported.

My wish to know what I will never know

is like being tossed
about in a washing machine,

trying to see out
the porthole.

Only an hour ago,

I was stuck like a car
the tires of which will only spin

in the happiness of eating a chicken egg

fried in the fat
of another animal, unaware

that there would be eclipse after eclipse,

as if waking itself
were the magnitude event

that the jittery heart, like a gyroscope,
accounts for,

so that we, like the athletes
we watch on television,
can regain and then maintain

a balance,
make the catch,

stay in bounds
voila!

Passing the laundromat (at Grand and 36th)

From the saddle of a bike, from which,
due to the speed and attention one must pay
to remain upright, I can only see so much.

A pair of brown socks

held above the basket
by a short gold woman

to the window
to see if they match

aren't socks
but the eyes of my grandmother.

She will write
in her journal,

as she waits for the machines,
that I am of indeterminate height,

fuzzy gray, crouched
like an ultrasound fetus.

The pair of blue socks
she holds up next

are crying.

The short gold woman
is a pupa

picking out wings.

Although the pavement below me
mirrors the surface of the moon

I am not wearing an astronaut suit
until she writes that I am.

The short woman and I
meeting at the eyes

make up a wishbone.

We will never see each other
                again.

ACKNOWLEDGMENTS

Iterations of these poems have appeared in *DIAGRAM, Sonora Review, Willow Springs, The Los Angeles Review, The World According to Goldfish, Vols. I & II, Tule Review,* and *Poetry Daily.* "The lullaby and well of night visit the day most memorably in things as resilient as wool" was a finalist in the Sonora Review Poetry Contest.

NOTES

Page 4 "Livin' on a Prayer" is Bon Jovi's second chart-topping single, from their third album, *Slippery When Wet.*

Page 42 The cop quotations come from the *SF Gate/San Francisco Chronicle* article "Cracking the Code of Silence" by Stephanie Salter (Sunday, March 9, 2003).

Page 45 The quotation *wandering forlorn of Paris once her playmate* is from Lord Alfred Tennyson's poem "'None.'"

AFTERWORD

"If you know my oeuvre" is a pretentious thing to say, I say having been nurtured by stoic Midwesterners for whom faith in the importance of humility is (or was) more widespread than faith in any god (a claim I'll stand by—*why not*), but I am going to say it nonetheless, because it is possible. So (here goes): If you know my oeuvre and read this new book, you will hear, as in an old house emptied of all save for its ghosts, echoes. You will experience the tiny and joyous rebirth that is deja vu. And this is not an accident. I have lived with some of the poems herein for nearly thirty years and have never stopped trying to get them right. It is a dance, the poems sometimes leading me and I sometimes leading them, and we are different, one to another, after each embrace, each go-round. I was a kind of Romeo, is a way to think of it, when the first published drafts of some of the poems here surfaced, and I am now older than Hamlet but not as old as Lear. I have shed and have acquired. Like a cornerback who cannot run as fast as he used to but is better at his job for the years of experience that allow him to react rather than think—those fractions of a second being all—I am presenting these echoes and this deja vu as veteran rather than rookie. I am blessed, that is, to do in part what Flannery O'Connor and Borges did, which is to present more realized versions of poems that I have presented before. I also have a better understanding of the ethos of my life in the times I have known, and am yet the same singular poet (though with less radiant flesh), whether I outwardly display as Romeo, Hamlet, or Lear, and so present side by side with the echoes and deja vu the very newest poems I have written, as well as poems that have been biding their time in various states of waiting and have finally gotten the call-up, all of which are, I can see now, kin, the strands wound together to make the book itself a single rope—something new.

One does not become who one becomes all on one's own, and neither do poems nor the books in which they find a shared residence. These poems and this book, in particular, are what they are due in no small part to the editorial guidance of Kyle McCord. This is not the manuscript I submitted. This is the book that Kyle's vision helped it become. And while we do not judge books by their covers, it is the cover which beckons us to pick a book from table or shelf, that leads to us paging through it and considering purchase. In this case, the stark image and design are thematic prelude to the poetry itself, and they would not be so if not for the machinations (of both artifact and its elements) of Nick Courtright, and the photography of Alec Soth. And as much I want you to find something in my poetry, I want you to find as well what I have found in Soth's photos. His official bio on his website will tell you that he "has had over fifty solo exhibitions including survey shows organized by Jeu de Paume in Paris, the Walker Art Center in Minnesota, and Media Space in London," that among his many awards is a Guggenheim Fellowship. I want you to explore his images, to buy his books, to subscribe to his wonderful Little Brown Mushroom newsletter, which is free, is a wonderful fusing of image and story that lands like an occasional gift from a stranger on the stoop that is your in-box.

This book has been finished during a pandemic, as cases and death tolls rise in what may well be only a first wave. I have spent my quarantine at a residence about seventeen blocks (closer as the crow, military drone, or national-guard chopper flies) from the Cup Foods where George Floyd was murdered and the world took notice. These things have entered into what this book has become. I am now a much more distilled kind of thankful for my butcher, my spirit shop, my two grocers, and my favorite local restaurants—and am a devout new enthusiast of curbside pickup. I am thankful for how a fertile college education helps me see and understand the times, for my colleagues, students, and staffs (at numerous places and in numerous ways) and the deep and astute thinkers on social media—for our pursuit of something that we hope tastes of wisdom and looks like justice, lifelong teachers and learners all. I miss the group of us who gathered under the auspices of composition pedagogy and instruction, but were really together for the wines, cheeses, and chatting, and I will be thankful to host us again (it's my turn) when this plague is gone. I am thankful for my bike-riding companion (in that and else) and our solemn, necessary, and masked visiting of the George Floyd memorial site at 38th and Chicago, and our daytime tour of the damage caused by the fires and riots in South Minneapolis in the last week of May 2020, the sounds and happening of which fell upon us like rain through the nights, as we damned the right-wing opportunists and agitators who flocked here in their license-plate-less trucks and cars and motorbikes to turn peaceful protests into their fiery and violent playground. I am thankful generally for the many good people of South Minneapolis, and Twin Cities wide for the justice protesters, artists, writers, thinkers, musicians, tryers, and doers. So many—too many—to name. If you think you see yourself here, you do.

I am thankful for my blurbers, who continue to help me see what I have done with clearer lenses. In my little, postage-stamp-sized urban backyard sanctuary, I am thankful for our (Angie's and mine) steeled international traveling companions, who have thrice now widened our perspective and most recently remained calm with us and the hundreds/thousands of others trying to return before the travel ban stranded us. I am thankful for my extended family, for our text thread and Zooms, and for my parents far enough away and old enough (one in a nursing home) that the pandemic has made the wise choice not visiting in person (especially to a pocket of the country—theirs— where the virus is deemed hoax and masks, etcetera, are scoffed at).

Angie, Cleo, and Charlie: We have been in our bubble for many months now. I am most thankful for us.

Thank you, too, to Monica for writing back. There are no pronghorns in Minneapolis, but that is thing: there are.

ABOUT THE AUTHOR

Matt Mauch is the author of four poetry collections, most recently, *Bird~Brain*. Founder of the Great Twin Cities Poetry Read and the journal *Poetry City*, his poems have appeared in numerous journals, including *Conduit, The Journal, DIAGRAM, Willow Springs, The Los Angeles Review, Forklift, Ohio, Sonora Review, Water~Stone Review,* and on the *Poetry Daily* and *Verse Daily* websites. His work has been recognized by the Minnesota State Arts Board and the National Poetry Series. Mauch lives in Minneapolis and teaches in the AFA in Creative Writing program at Normandale Community College.

CPSIA information can be obtained
at www.ICGtesting.com
Printed in the USA
FSHW010833240421